Kitchen Table Midwife of the Dispossessed

poems by

Ruth Mota

Finishing Line Press
Georgetown, Kentucky

Kitchen Table Midwife
of the Dispossessed

ACKNOWLEDGMENTS

Many thanks to the editors of the following journals for first publishing
some of the poems included in this chapbook:

Passager Books: Women Cooking Chicken
Moonstone Press: Ode to the Beet, At the Yuma Border Facility, Evening
Song
The Nature of Our Times: Water Lessons
The Word's Faire: A Family Carnaval, Fava Memories of a Kitchen Midwife
The Gyroscope Review: Eggplant Consummation
Hare's Paw: Mercy, The Fury of Garlic
Caesura: Capiberibe Bridge, Nowruz
Waxing and Waning: For Hind Rajab
Quillsedge Press: Billie's Brazilian Ghost
Reservoir Road: In the Asylum Among Us Crazies
Isotrope Literary Magazine, Discordant Symphony
Stonecoast Review: Recife
Fourth River Literary Journal: Birthing at the Center of the Earth

Much gratitude for inspirational and editorial support from Ellen Bass,
Magdalena Montagne, Susan Giddings, Juanita Usher, Sheila Siegel and
Maria Ponciano.

Publisher: Leah Huete de Maines
Editor: Christen Kincaid
Cover Art: Ruth Mota
Author Photo: Sarojani Rohan
Cover Design: Elizabeth Maines McCleavy

Order online: www.finishinglinepress.com
also available on amazon.com

Author inquiries and mail orders:
Finishing Line Press
PO Box 1626
Georgetown, Kentucky 40324
USA

Contents

Women Cooking Chicken

How unlike the chicken of my youth these thighs and breasts
severed, wrapped in cellophane and labeled *cage-free*.
Spared the sight of blood and scent of ripened flesh,
I only need a quick hot-wash to plop my pullet in the pan.

At thirteen, my first chicken came without a pedigree
blanketed in plain pink paper from Ducca's Butcher Shop.
Confronted by a whole chicken, except for head and feet
I felt her featherless skin erupting just like mine.

I laid her naked on her back across the cutting board
shoved my hand through the hole between her legs
to retrieve her heart, a twisted neck, whatever *giblets* were.
My mother put me to this task without instruction,
so my blade landed many cuts before I clipped her joints
divided body parts I dusted and dunked in sizzling oil.

So many women in the world have slaughtered chickens.
I saw a sugar-cane farmer's wife on a plantation in Brazil
chase a chicken with her machete to slit its throat.
She wrapped her legs ribboned with purple veins
around a bucket of scalding water to pluck its feathers.
That tough old hen who pecked for scratch would never
sizzle in a frying pan, but boil for hours to feed a family.
Its claws afloat, yesterday's bread sopping up its juice.

As I lay my platter down now upon my table
and watch my daughters' greasy fingers fiddle
with crispy thighs and breasts, I wonder how,
when they are women, they will relate to chickens?
Will they find it too grotesque to touch such flesh?
Or will a uniformed woman wrapping in a factory
make their slaughtered poultry palatable?

Eggplant Consummation

I am drawn to how the purple robe
of the eggplant glistens like a bruise

how, as a royal bride, she succumbs to my blade
her coat curling down onto my cutting board.

I admire how she reveals her spongy white flesh
puffy as eyelids after a good cry

in my therapist's chair where I've cut
through to another bitter truth.

When I sprinkle salt on her severed rings
she will cry too, drops rising from her limp rounds.

I dry her tears, snow her with flour. Bless her
with the blood of tomatoes, the iridescence of onions.

I cede her to the sizzling oil of my pan, life consecrated
then consumed down my dark throat to another universe.

Ode to the Beet

The beet resists
clenching earth
with its tenacious drill
as my fist tightens.
I tug it from the dark cave
of its winter dreams
towards the sun.
Its tap dug deep
like a syringe sucking
loam-life up into its
bulbous purple belly—
an organ manly and unshaven,
fragrant with dirt
that blankets my palms and
paints black-moon slivers
beneath my nails.
Waxen stems fan
to scalloped green leaves
veined in violet.
Even before the butter
melts in my pan, where onions
simmer to the translucence of ghosts,
those sweet leaves tantalize my tongue
while its engorged belly-heart
bleeds its rage into my pot.

The Fury of Garlic

Bring the bulb to my table.
Rub your thumb over its bearded belly.
Let your finger caress its papery old-man skin
as it sloughs off in your palm
to reveal a ring of ivory teeth
agape like the jaw of a feral beast,
its fetid breath warding off curses and plagues.

Curses and plagues,
as in the Middle Ages, have come again
afloat in air or seeping out of silver screens,
drooling from our politicians' mouths.
We summoned them through ignorance and cruelty.
If only a garlic wreath wrapped in wool
could help protect us now.

But you, my friend, believe in science.
You relish garlic for its allicin
its antibiotic, antifungal attributes
that lower pressure and your LDL.
Imagine instead, fires along our street tonight—
garlic thrown in flames as it was in ancient Borneo
with pleas to conjure souls we lost so long ago.

Mercy

Come into my kitchen—listen
to acorn bowling, nail scratching,
secrets whispered behind walls—see

tucked in the dark alley by my fridge
three gnawed tangerines, a blue scouring sponge,
chewed foil glittering like starlight.

When the tea water whistles, that dark snake slithers
in my belly and my mother appears enveloped in steam
clenching her shovel. Bang, bang

like our screen door in the wind, the pointed tip
decapitates a pink litter of curled mice—dumped
from their fluffy nest in a copper kettle onto cold stone

and the Afghani child—ribs rising like railroad tracks—
stares into space, her body a flaccid kidney arranged
on a mottled blanket, gasping for mercy.

Nowruz

Drum-roll on my metal roof
a downpour announces spring.
Redwoods stir a dome of gray
while across the world from California
you buy goldfish in the market of Tehran
arrange apples and hyacinths on a Persian cloth.

I celebrate earth's rebirth with you.
In distant kitchens we resurrect
the mischievous wisdom of Hafiz,
scenes from the master's verse painted on eggs:
a singer under stars, a sage dropping keys,
a thirsty fish perched upon a camel.

You and I yearn for friendship
yet wonder what became of our two cultures
and what size mushroom will blossom in this rain.

For Hind Rajab

I knead bread
my palms pressing its girth
my knuckles curling into its acquiescent flesh
that cedes to my sorrow
surging today after they found
next to the ashes of the Red Crescent ambulance
her six-year-old body, her voice still,
still on the phone after three hours
calling for help from the car
where her family lay silent beside her
when she pleaded to cease this fire
that engulfed them.

I need rage
my fingers white with flour
so as not to get stuck here
but to keep kneading, moving forward
molding dough to a different future.
I braid it like the thick hair of a fallen child.
Bed it in my oven and wait for it to rise,
to fill my kitchen with the scent
of nourishment and shame.

Water Lessons

Once as a child, at my kitchen sink,
I watched water gush from our faucet,
its steam engulfing me,
its thrust bubbling my dish soap.   .
I marveled at its abundant glistening stream
that seemed an endless glow of silver light.

I wondered how this liquid,
hot for cleansing, cold for thirst,
obedient to each subtle twist of wrist,
how such a precious thing as water could be free?
What if we had to pay for it like milk that arrived
in bottles weekly at our door!

Of course, I did not know about my parents' water bill.
I did not know this water came from high in the Sierras,
a valley named Hetch-Hetchy, a grass that fed the Miwok.
Did not know what it cost the Miwok to flood their valley,
robbed of home, community, their link to spirit world,
so this water could flow through pipes to fill my sink.

I knew my water came in pipes, but did not know that all
water does not come in pipes—how many women in the world
must carry water on their heads from wells and rivers
or make their living washing clothes along some muddy bank
where flukes from snails that sailed on slave ships
can turn their urine red, make their kidneys fail.

Later I learned how water is abused and must be treated.
How it is polluted, hoarded, stolen from the dispossessed.
How this war we're funding now is fought for gas and water.
Water, not an endless flow, but finite like our life.
So much in childhood I did not know,
yet even in unknowing at that moment by my sink,
watching water flow, I sensed its sanctity.

Fava Memories of a Kitchen Midwife

Today I harvested our fava beans.
I slide my thumbnail down their seams.
Fold back their green wings to retrieve
the embryos nestled in that spongy white.
Slick skin slithers through my fingers
falls plinking to the colander below.
I am midwife at my kitchen table.
My daughters grown, their daughters grown.
My white hair dusted with tiny purple petals.
Before me, a mound of empty shells.

Gathering these, I remember the fazenda in Brazil
where I first saw fava beans. The farmer's wife
who taught the one-room school there,
kept her husband's books at his bodega,
raised their twenty children, mostly grown and gone,
tossed fava from her woven sieve like swirling birds
into the golden twilight beneath the shadow of a palm.
She watched her chaff be carried by the breeze,
her reflection so palpable I could enter it,
as if we measured life in fava beans.
Was it worth it? Where had it gone?
Light-distant. Womb heavy.

Bridge Over the Capiberibe

I remember the night those March rains ended
when we crossed together over the swollen Capiberibe.
Recife's ripened scent wrapped round us in a muggy shawl.
Moonlight mirrored contorted in the swirling muddy water
while in the shadows, crabbers clinked and scurried below.

A beggar jangled coins in the bottom of his Nestle can.
His eyes pierced me as he yelled: *Alema, me da dinheiro!*
We pass him by, I pretend not to hear; you don't hear
too worried about the days before your next paycheck
about our car in the body-shop, the baby in my belly.

Sweat beads on your brow as you see the coins in your palm
and realize we have just enough to catch the bus home
while I find it miraculous our monetary salvation is so precise.
Your worries block this city's pain. I absorb it:
the woman digging in our garbage, legs swollen and scabbed,
the boy who twirled the latch on my purse when he ran by
the latch you reminded me to turn inward towards my breast.

On that bridge we walked together
but tumbling in different dreams:
you afraid of sliding into poverty,
me calming the upheaval in my soul
where the stench of injustice kept rising,
turgid and brown like the river below.

Birthing at the Center of the Earth

The ageless midwife of the Amazon
clothes herself in white when she is summoned.
Wet season now. No paths to climb—
all her world a womb of water.
Steady at the oar, she glides round lily pads
large as heliports to the birthing mother's stilted house.

Arara¸ arara…macaws announce
she has arrived for the thousandth time
each visit marked like bird-scratch
painted on her hands.
The men dismissed, she settles in
between the spreading thighs.
Watch how her fingers knotted
as the roots of ceiba trees slide
round the uterus, swivel the wandering babe
to the entrance of that slippery cave.

The midwife soothes with songs of the *Tupi*
as she cooks and cleans, then kneads a belly.
They wait. No rushing, no appointed hour.
Let life enter on its own time.
Let the new one come cascading
like the river into earthen palms
emerging under howls, his tethered cord bit free
by teeth that glimmer in the firelight.

Billie's Brazilian Ghost

We hear your plaintive call
echoes of *Yemanja*, goddess of the sea
succor to women in child-birth
to grandmothers cutting cane
to young girls whose bellies rise
before their breasts have blossomed.

Your rhythm pulses in umber legs
a heel grazing a cheekbone—
quick crouch and a cartwheel
capoeira death moves masked as dance
dreaming of a ruptured jugular.
Your harmony limber as the foot of a thief
who steps over shards of glass rising from a stucco wall,
lithe as barefoot boys on the beach
who transform soccer balls to acrobats and comets.

Fire lilies unfurl from your throat
blooming in a voice laden with ash.
Champagne bubbles rise in a smoke-filled room.
Chains creak in a service elevator for a diva descending.
Click of handcuffs on your deathbed
heard by ghosts in holds of galleons.

Oh Billie, raise your voice just one more time.
Let Bahia's concert halls conjure poplars
where we pray strange fruit will never hang again.

Fontainha

Just where Brazil raises its hunched back towards Africa,
there lies a beach called Fontainha rippled with dunes and
amber sandstone cliffs. At dawn, teams of fishermen guide
their *jangadas* over the waves. One man stands by the mast,
a white sail fluttering beside him. Another on the wooden bench
at the stern guides his boat towards shore. Five crafts float like
a flock of gulls. As soon as they cross the last breaker, the men
jump into the foam. Women and children greet them, curious
about their haul. Sailors roll their boats over logs to shore.

At the edge of a cliff, a lone woman
braces herself against whipping wind
her black skirt soaring like a vulture's wing.

Arm cocked, she shields her eyes from the sun's glare
and scans the horizon where pink and gold meet blue.
She plants herself, stiff as steel, only her dress in motion.

The fishermen remove their sails and spread their rafts
along the beach. They hoist up woven baskets and cast
their catch across a tarp: piles of slithering silver mackerel,
glittering pink perch, black-spotted grouper with bulging
eyes and gaping, grumpy mouths. Around the spread of fish,
barefoot boys line up with fathers. Excitedly they wait
for today's choices to be wrapped in yesterday's news.
Fish scent is caught by the wind, stirred by swaying palms.
carried up the dunes to the big white house upon the hill.

Folks in the high house rub their eyes, stretch in hammocks.
They rise, enticed by coffee wafting from the kitchen, but
bothered by the odor drifting up the hill from down below.

The woman in black on the sandstone cliff remains, but
no longer alone. Three children huddle round her as she's
folded on the ground, head bowed, arms clutching knees.

First Feijoada
National Dish of Brazil

Workweek done and masters fed,
cook's wooden spoon still makes
black beans dance a samba rout
in the belly of a big black pot.
Boiling pigs' feet kick a curly tail
and other swirling porcine rejects
from the rich folk's house.

A severed ear cocks up from spicy sauce
as if to catch the cadence of the drums.
Cook's line of daughters busy by her side
imbibe that rhythm too as they season rice
peel papery skin from garlic teeth,
cleaver up the collard greens, sizzle sandy
mounds of manioc in spitting grease.
Slice a pile of bright orange cartwheels
to cut their way through salty fat.

Men, returned from slashing cane, have stolen rum.
Boys pick limes and the meal's complete
when they birth a *caipirinha*.
Music mixes with the soupy scent
of beans and meat—sails in cumin clouds
from squat row houses to the *Casa Grande*
where powdered ladies and lace-cuffed men
sit in high-back chairs and measure sugar
from an unlocked silver bowl into tiny coffee cups.

The flavor of their country's future pride arrives
but sated from the loin, finer cuts of meat
and far, far lighter beans, they try to feign
those succulent scents come throbbing
onto their veranda do not entice.

A Family Carnaval

Fat Tuesday on the veranda.
  Primo Lino strums his cavaquinho.
    Guitars riff. Agogo' bongs. Drums pound.
      The cuica squeaks, as elders croon.
        Barefoot kids hook a caterpillar chain
      that kicks its thirty legs in samba-sync
    and weaves it way through revelers.
Seu Ribamar's big bronze belly flashes gold medallions
    as he swivels to the patio floor with me
      while maiden aunts swirl unleashed, hands in sway
       above their heads like palm fronds.
    Tios Chico and Liborio in a duel, to wager who can dance
  the longest balancing a beer upon his head.
The scent of feijoada rises from the kitchen
    where Dona Quinquinha stirs ham hocks and beans
until another drunk uncle bursts in,
    sashays her across the blue-tiled floor,
        laughter flowing back outside.
    Fishermen's kids surround the porch in ragged shorts
  kick up feathery whirls of sand with spinning moves.
When night descends, only the moon is still
    its gleaming eye silent and unblinking
      over waves that tow our footfalls out to sea.

Saudades

Colatina, Brasil

After you abandon the *favela* I drive up the hill.
A dozen dust-covered boys shout my name in Portuguese
at our powder-blue jeep: *Dona Hoochie! Dona Hoochie!*
You told me they yelled my name at you too when you drove.
Was that why you left?

In our shack I see a stack of unwashed dishes,
hear the echoes of your laughter from when Lucita
stood by our gleaming pots exclaiming how well my
white tampons worked as scrubbers.
Too tired for dishes, to build a fire, to boil water,
I bathe in the cold metal basin. I miss your voice
reading Gabriela while you waited your turn.
But Eva, we alternated who went first.

Our gigantic jealous neighbor doesn't rage tonight
but your eyes alit with fear still float in my mind—
from the time her husband cried: *Larga esta faca, mulher!*
Thuds, crash of furniture resound through plywood walls.
I never asked which one you thought was stabbed
before they called out in despair: *Volta para Deus!*
If we'd fought, would we return to God?

The days pass quickly. Today I laid bricks at school,
took feces to the lab, planted squash with the soccer team.
It's the nights that last long, thick with *saudades*,
mice scratching in the cupboard, a distant guitar.
My fingers smoothe the orange tablecloth
we bought together at the fabric shop

Instructions on Roofing in Brazil

He above, straddles a stallion.
The brim of his leather hat tilts right
as he critiques the wooden frame the villagers
have woven and packed with mud.
Sweeping his arm, he proclaims: *The walls look solid.*
Just throw some palm leaves for a roof.
I below am blinded by the light behind him
and his horse who snorts approval of his master's wisdom.
After he saunters off, I stand outside the door beside a pile
of palm leaves fanning out across the plot.
I've never thrown a palm leaf. What is there but to try?

The men have done their part. Now the women come
up from the river smelling of laundry soap and sweat.
We settle in a circle—legs crossed in the dust—
leaves three meters long spread out before us.
I mimic their nimble moves, press the fronds onto the ground.
We pull the top ones down to rest parallel with their mate.
Edges, sharp as piranhas' teeth, cut my fingers before I climb
to bind the stems like giant fish vertebra on the beams.
He appears again, below this time, at the height of my task.
He's hatless now, off his high horse but still a swagger in his step.
Eyeing my bloody fingers, he says: *You must fold the palms?*

Recife

In Recife, million-strong metropolis
that points its Brazilian nose at Africa,
on an avenue named for a famous baron
so rich he owned eight sugar cane plantations,
so important his namesake links an airport
to the lapping green waves of the Atlantic.
In the very middle of that street
flanked by a pair of graviola trees
protected by thick stucco walls
that menace with claws of jagged glass
sat my little blue house.

Mornings, wheeling the stroller,
I escaped from its filigreed bars into that equatorial heat
where bare-chested, bare-foot boys dashed past me
as I walked towards the home of the silver-bellied planes
where the shops were air-conditioned and
soldiers in polished black boots guarded them
with machine guns and lascivious smirks
to where my toddler would learn to walk
and could watch the sad-eyed manatee swim
round and round a tiny palm-lined pond.

Evenings, when the baby slept
when the cool night air descended like a prayer,
I walked away from the honking VW bugs,
the smoke of overloaded buses, walked alone
to the pulsing sea to sing songs of moonrise on the desert
where a host of rats rose from among the jagged rocks
their beady eyes transfixed by my melancholy melody,
an entire chorus line of them, paws poised on tummies
heads cocked as if they conjured the moment
I would lead them away.

In the Asylum Among Us Crazies

a caterpillar crawls from its pink shell.
I don't know what impelled it to be born.
Perhaps its sixteen legs were cramped.
Or was it hungry for a jambu leaf?
Its bulbous head emerges as it chews
its way to face this world.

In the courtyard Alexis lights another cigarette
oblivious to its birth on the branch above her.
She only sees the ghost of her lost love not me, her friend,
nor the sorrowful eyes of her husband come
to bring her ironed clothes and a bottle of shampoo.

Gummy black bristles sprout round a bulbous body.
A squirming brush, filaments spray from tips, detect danger.
Done with its dark mask, two legs peel it back like a helmet.
Reveal a jelly-green bubble of a face, a humungous mouth
designed to devour all the green around it.

One gnawed leaf falls on Sargent Lino
the cop who tortured seventeen subversives.
He trembles at the thought of electric shock.
Hopes no one hears the screams that echo in his skull
as he stares in stupor at a buzzing blizzard on TV.

The caterpillar, bright white now, twists snowflakes in the heat
until it sheds its coat then eats it. Its new skin blue and green
with two orange circles underneath. Curling in a desiccated leaf
it spins a tawny nest, a cocoon to rest, a silken purse of fashion.

Dona Yara, that silver-haired lady with rattling teeth
once a famous pianist, hidden in our ward by her rich sisters
will never use that purse. Not ever. Nor will Lourdes,
the raven-haired beauty who saw her daughter floating in a tank.
They cannot see the silk cocoon from the dreaded second floor
where the steely-eyed nurse threatens to send us all forever.

The Atlas Moth arises in angelic and demonic splendor.
Her massive wings unfold—one entire foot across.
Blood-orange seas with sailboats afloat upon them.
Snowy mountain edges. Two golden snakes above.
Her voracious caterpillar mouth is gone. She cannot feed.
A life so fleeting, but look how she completes her journey
from beast to beauty free from shame or any moral compass.

The Gardener

I met you on that sweltering January day
at my Recife house—the blue one on Sousa Leão—
my daughter pedaling her tricycle under our grape arbor
my belly bursting with her sister.
The garden overgrown with twisted vines of passion fruit
purple jambos hanging heavy like dark hearts
grass so high it hid my swollen ankles.
You startled me at the gate with those pruning shears.
Your open shirt threadbare, parched of color, revealed
a chest beaded with sweat. You asked if I needed help.
It was years ago so I expect you've forgotten that day
and the weeks you came to prune and water
shy and diligent, leaving with bags of fruit
and my husband's shirts mixed in with your wages

I told you we'd be gone for the weekend but didn't tell you
friends would come to stay, who heard footsteps on the roof
the clamor of tiles, then saw how the sudden light scared you
and you climbed the wall embedded with shards of glass.
Not until the rains returned and water drizzled on our bed
did we see how close you came to entering.
The grass grew back. I never saw you again.
Felt a fool for hiring you, for examining your ragged shirt
rather than your sly eyes, for not catching how you cased
our locks and window-bars to plan your rooftop plot.
But even as betrayal stung, I saw your point.
Gifts of harvest would never heal the breach between us.
A problem of this size needs root removal.
Within two years I hovered in the aisle of a plane
as my children slept, as we fled forever that bolted house
to meet again the hungry in my old hometown.

Kalinda and the Killing Fields

It was my mistake, the wrong movie.
I thought The Killing Fields was a farming flick.
Please understand. I wouldn't have intentionally
subjected my daughter, at only thirteen,
to the violence of the Khmer Rouge...
all those guns pointed the wrong way
bullets spraying through the theater
towards her beautiful brown face.

Her sobbing lasted for months like her rage
at her parents who couldn't understand this was real.
Real like the ragged men ejected from mental wards
who began to appear on the street corners of University Ave,
men not yet labeled *the homeless*, just scruffy
unshaven guys with plastic bags and hungry stares,
men I refused to stop for, because
we couldn't be late to her bassoon lesson.

Why didn't adults, the ones with the power, do something?
It made her sick. She stopped eating. Her ribs showed.
At the Co-Op, I coaxed her to choose foods she liked.
She took me to the bins out back, to *the perfectly good food*
piled in the dumpster: cans of beans and tuna with small dents,
day-old bread, pasta barely past the expiration date.
At sixteen she showed us, crammed our Buick with six men.
While her friend's parents vacationed in Hawaii, they
cooked a meal with food from the Co-Op dumpster.
She said the men were shy, seemed grateful, smelled bad.
The worried mom, I checked the paper for news of botulism.
None of that, but Haing Ngor, star in The Killing Fields,
who wasn't really an actor, but a doctor tortured by Pol Pot,
won an Oscar before he was shot in an L.A. parking lot.

Discordant Symphony

It isn't the gray of cracked concrete or the upturned asphalt
or even the smell of piss that makes this city sad.
It's the sounds: jackhammers, car-horns, sirens
repeated *fuck yous* from a guy wrapped in a blanket
a defiant "I *am* drugs!" shouted towards our table.
Because of covid we eat outdoors so this cacophony splatters
on my husband's honey-baked chicken, over my pumpkin pie.
It's a wretched overture to the music we've come to hear.

Near the concert hall she catches my eye, a young woman
pretty in her frayed beige sweater striped with pink.
She's done something to her hair that takes a good mirror.
So, I'm surprised when she says she's homeless.
I nod when she asks. She waits as I fumble in my purse
then place a twenty in her hand. We touch each other's
shame ignited by a lady in stilettos eyeing our exchange.

The crowd pushes me away from her towards the border
where we must show: ID, tickets, vaccination cards.
I sit in the center of the third row of this other country.
The seat in front of me empty, I save it for her.
Imagine watching the orchestra over the waves of her hair.
Am curious what she would think of the famous Bronfman
who is slumped over the Steinway, hair a tangled gray bush
looking frumpy and rumpled as Beethoven himself.
Bronfman wouldn't see her. He sees nothing, listens
to the cello's queries, answers with sweet trills, like a
dialogue I want to have with her after the concert.

How would she react to the velvet hammers in front of her
caressing her cheek or pounding rage at life's injustice?
The bassoonist in the Strauss, would she adore him too?
See the twinkle in his eye, water sprite of sparkling pendant,
whose fingers flit like butterflies over clinking silver keys.
Would she be thrilled by her rescue from the din of cussing?
Or would she fall sleep like the person beside me?

At the Yuma Border Facility

Sobbing fills the room.
It spirals along wires crowned in thorns.
Feet swollen, throat parched, she waits for hours
in the coiling line. How can one day be so long?
How can thirst be so deep that she drinks from a toilet?

El llanto llena la sala,
rodea arriba por cables coronados de espinas.
Sus pies hinchados, su garganta reseca,
ella espera por horas en la fila serpentina.
¿Como es posible un día tan largo o una sed
tan profunda que ella bebe el agua del inodoro?

Finally the moon rises, frozen eyeball that never blinks,
that spreads its icy stare over the stone floor
where her sisters curl together like shivering kittens.
She'll stand watch. If she sleeps, she'll dream
of the mocking laughter, the guard's fat fingers
between her thighs.

Finalmente la luna nace, globo de ojo que nunca parpadea,
que extiende su mirada congelada sobre el piso de piedra
donde sus hermanas se acurrucan como gatitas temblorosas.
Ella mantendrá la vigilancia. Si durmiera, seguro soñará
con las risas burlonas, los dedos gordos del guardia
entre sus muslos.

They Keep Coming

These children. They invade my sleep, sometimes
hundreds at once waiting patiently for soup at a table
so long their brown faces at the end look like thumbs.
Chased by soldiers, they follow me under thunder.
Their numbers fade till I reach an abyss cradling just one.
I must decide whether to be caught or jump into the void.
I leap, but float, look back. Storm over. Soldiers gone.
The cliff, a field of daisies bathed in light.
I fall and land in soft gray mud, the babe become a ball.

The kids are often fluid like that in number or in essence
like the baby giraffe who gallops into the living room
where I lie naked under white sheets while the rest of my
book club sits in a circle discussing the book I haven't read.
His hooves click against the hardwood floor before he slips
beneath the covers, wraps his reticulated neck across my chest.
Hot breath from his nostrils pulse against my cheek. I worry
he's far from his savannah, but I must use the bathroom.
He follows me. Makes no sound, though his anguish
at our separation oozes through the door. When I open,
he's become an angel, blazing a newborn's face.

Tonight, I am encircled by a group of women clothed in chador.
I want them to share their verse, but they refuse
to give their names. One says to call her #782 before she yells:
Don't you get it! then thrusts an infant in my face.
In the light of morning, they keep coming.
I awaken to a girl's plea at the El Paso border.
She repeats the prayer her mamacita said would save her:
Call my aunt. Her number is 324 6198.
Her tiny fists pound the floor inside a circle of guards
clad in blue-cloth covered shoes.

Evening Song

In the quiet of an iris
undulating bed of purple,
I will my heart to settle
to nest in petals and disremember
the raucous cawing of this day
stench and crackle, dry death rattle
of blessed mother earth.

The cascading coos of mourning doves
weave above my silence and I wonder
could this be their last song?
When will come the last song
of the last bird on our planet?
Are there other worlds with other birds
to take up your melancholy tune?

Ever since I watched our galaxy
stretch and swallow stars,
I lost faith in forever.
It will have to be enough that your mourning
echoes through the air this evening—
that once, for a moment
there was such a thing as beauty,
and we entered it.

Grace

Take me sun
as you do the yellow tulip
who unfolds her cup each morning
to drink your mana.

Cover me Sun
like loam's warm blanket.
Seep down to my roots, spread
your golden threads from womb to toe.

Fill my mind
emptied of thought
with your crimson tunnel—sweet throat—
that swallows all the shadows of my sins.

Ruth Mota currently lives in Santa Cruz, California, with her Brazilian husband. Previously she resided nearly a decade in northeast Brazil and worked as an international HIV/AIDS trainer throughout Africa and Latin America. She was first drawn to Spanish language and culture when she heard a Spaniard read from Lorca's *Bodas de Sangrre* in her English class at Oberlin College. Lorca's passion continues to resonate with her as she reflects on her diverse experiences with dispossessed people at her kitchen table.